# A More Urgent Season

Sermons And Children's Lessons
For Thanksgiving, Advent,
Christmas and Epiphany Sunday

## Erskine White

CSS Publishing Company, Inc.
Lima, Ohio

*BV40
.W46
1993*

Copyright © 1993 by
The CSS Publishing Company, Inc.
Lima, Ohio

---

**Library of Congress Cataloging-in-Publication Data**

White, Erskine, 1951-
    A more urgent season : sermons and object lessons for Advent, Christmas, and Epiphany / by Erskine N. White.
        p.     cm.
    ISBN 1-55673-654-1
    1. Advent sermons. 2. Christmas sermons. 3. Epiphany season — Sermons. 4. Sermons, American. I. Title.
BV40.W46      1993
252'.61—dc20                                                      93-18005
                                                                      CIP

---

9354 / ISBN 1-55673-654-1                    PRINTED IN U.S.A.

## Dedication

This book is lovingly dedicated to the men, women and children of the new Christian community which the Holy Spirit brought together and sustained for a crucial time in Melrose, Massachusetts. We passed through the fiery furnace together and came out unsinged. We exposed works of darkness together and learned deep lessons of faith. Words like "Thank you" and "We love you" are completely inadequate.

> — *Erskine, Caroline, Daniel,*
> *Joshua and Jordan White*

# Table Of Contents

## A Word About Language

The language in this book pertaining to people is inclusive of men and women. Similarly, the anecdotes and illustrations have been deliberately varied so as to include the experiences of women and men alike. As for the language pertaining to God, I have used pronouns (generally "He" for God and "She" for the Holy Spirit) in order to preserve the biblical insistence that ours is a personal God. Whenever it appears, however, the pronoun is always initiated with a capital "H" (or "S"), indicating to the reader that God is neither male nor female in human terms.

*— E.W.*

# Introduction

In introducing an earlier volume of Advent sermons *(Some Assembly Required,* published by CSS in 1989), I spoke of the difficulty facing seasoned preachers who must try to tell the familiar Christmas story in new and interesting ways year after year. The emphasis in those earlier sermons was on innovation and variety — a diverse array of homiletical styles, structures and substance was offered in the hope that colleagues in the pulpit might find an idea, an approach, or even just an anecdote which would help enrich their own Advent preaching.

In some ways, this present book mirrors that earlier effort at variety and is offered in the same spirit. For example, one sermon tells the imaginary tale of the angel Gabriel's skeptical cousin, Hector. Other sermons range in tone from a fanciful discussion of pregnancy to a frank discussion of peace. The artistic highlight of the book is a "Once upon a time" story sermon set in the make-believe land of Cornucopia, while another sermon draws a radically prophetic vision of Christmas through the eyes of two biblical women. To remain fresh through succeeding Advent seasons, preachers must try to stretch themselves in as many different directions as possible.

In other ways, however, this present book reflects a more evolved understanding of the complexities of Advent preaching. With increasing experience comes the recognition that innovation and sermonic variety are only part of the preacher's Advent challenge; additionally, there are deeper pastoral and theological nuances which must be juxtaposed and held in dialectical tension if the Advent message is to be fully and authentically presented.

In pastoral terms, preachers must pay attention to the emotional ambiguities and incongruities of the Christmas season, since many of their parishioners will approach the holidays with decidedly mixed feelings. In truth, most people are lonely, lost or wounded in one way or another by the exigencies of life, and they will feel those pains more acutely at Christmas time because they contrast so pointedly with the holiday good cheer which is relentlessly marketed by the secular culture.

To be sure, people want to hear "tidings of comfort and joy" at this time of year, and readers will find such tidings amply expressed in these pages, for they must always remain the irreplaceable core of the Christmas story. But people also hunger for constructive honesty from their preachers, and a recognition from the pulpit that the mixed feelings which trouble their hearts at Christmas time are understandably a part of the faithful Christian's Advent journey. As suggested a moment ago, the secular culture has a commercial agenda during the holiday season which tends to deny and suppress such emotional ambivalencies; people who yearn for more spiritual candor and a fuller expression of the whole range of their human experience will turn to the Christian preacher to find it.

In addition to such pastoral ambiguities, the preacher must also pay attention to the theological ambiguities of the Advent-Christmas-Epiphany season. Briefly stated, Christ's birth is properly anticipated and celebrated at three interacting levels. First, there is the historical event of His birth at a specific place and time, an event which incarnated God's love and made possible the universal salvation ultimately won at the empty tomb. Second, there is the spiritual "rebirth" of Jesus every year at Christmas time, sung in carols and acted out in pageants, an annual opportunity for Christians to hear the herald angels sing and renew their devotion to their newborn King. If such a categorization is not too simplistic, it can be said that these first two levels of Advent celebration are generally concerned with the past and present respectively.

However, Advent also has a definite futuristic focus, a strong eschatological anticipation of Christ's return to fully redeem a world which "did not know Him" when "the Word became flesh and lived among us." (John 1:10, 14) This third aspect of Advent theology becomes ever-more important as the sensitive Christian conscience grows increasingly disturbed by the gaping contrast between the ideals of peace, justice, love and hope which permeate the prophetic aspect of the Christmas message and the actual conditions of violence, injustice, discord and despair which permeate the contemporary world. Given these pervasive, unholy realities, part of the preacher's annual challenge is to fearlessly illumine this oft-neglected social dimension of Advent, to enlist Christian energies in the struggle for what is just, pure and true, and to anticipate the day when Christ shall return to redeem this sorely afflicted world in the fullness of time.

The apostle Paul charged preachers to be "urgent in season and out of season;" (2 Timothy 4:2) in no season is this exhortation more important than at Christmas time, when secular and scriptural sensibilities are most vocally and visibly at odds. Thus, if there is one theme which ties the disparate tones and styles of these sermons together, it is the call for genuine Christian conversion and commitment in response to God's gift, the birth of His Son. Sometimes this call is issued subtly and other times more explicitly, but it remains in these pages a consistent and unifying theme for the Thanksgiving-Advent-Christmas-Epiphany season.

Indeed, there is a palpable hunger in our land today for change, as people search for values and moral meaning in their individual lives, and as society seeks to recover functional ethical moorings in its institutional life. Advent offers a natural homiletical entry point for addressing this hunger in both personal and social terms. The civil religion which guides secular society and the cultural religion which guides too much of the established church are inadequate to the task of spiritual regeneration; biblical spirituality alone can fill the empty places. Given the Christian imperatives involved, faithful preaching rooted in scripture will strive to make Advent a more urgent season than perhaps it formerly has been. It will rise up and boldly say that Jesus Christ is born in our midst to show us the way, that the new life we so desperately seek and no less urgently need is at hand.

*Erskine White*
*Asheville, North Carolina*
*August, 1992*

Thanksgiving Day Sunday

# What To Give The God Who Has Everything

**Psalm 50:7-15**
**"Make thanksgiving your sacrifice to God ..."**
**(v. 14)**

With Thanksgiving near and Christmas not far behind, I wonder if any of you have people who are very difficult to shop for, people for whom it is very difficult to decide what to give. The two hardest people on my shopping list were always my grandparents. Especially as the years went by, I found myself asking, "What do you give to people who already have everything?" New sweaters or potholders or neckties didn't mean very much, since they were already amply supplied. A new book might be nice, but they already had plenty of books, and a new book didn't seem very creative anyway. It was very hard to decide what to give them.

I'll tell you how we solved the problem in our family. My grandfather was completely bald, so one of his presents every year was a new hairbrush. (Once in a while we climbed out of our rut and gave him some shampoo instead.) As for my grandmother, I think one of the best gifts she ever received came on her 90th birthday. We took pictures of all her grandchildren and their families and had them mounted in a frame. I do believe she appreciated that simple present more than many others she had been given over the years.

What gifts can we give to God? That's a far more perplexing question than we ever face with our friends or relatives, and it happens to be the subject of our text today. Do we even think about what we might give God at this or any other time of year? We often list the things God could give us to make us happy (like better health or the winning lottery number or even world peace), but how often do we think about what we could give God to make Him happy?

The idea of giving gifts to God may seem absurd in one sense, but the reality is that God's people have always done it on a regular basis. Israel offered sacrificial bulls and goats when they gathered for worship. Today, we offer the sacrifice of a portion of our money and lay it on the altar each week. Our text says that God doesn't rebuke Israel for these sacrifices (v. 8a), any more than He rebukes us for our gifts of money, which, He says, "are continually before Me." (v. 8b) But God goes on to say, in effect, "Let's keep this business of gift-giving in perspective."

"After all," God says to Israel, "What are you giving Me when you sacrifice an animal or a bird? Every creature who walks the earth is Mine, and I know all the birds who fly in the air, so what are you doing but giving me what I already own? Therefore, I don't want these burnt offerings from you."

(This, by the way, is one example of how the new Bible translation [the NRSV] is much superior to the old RSV. The old Bible translates verse 9 of our text: "I will accept no bull from your house." Now, a phrase like that has taken on quite a different meaning in this day and age, so the new Bible reads, "I will not accept a bull from your house." Just one of the finer points of modern biblical scholarship I thought you might like to know.)

At any rate, when God says that everything in heaven and on earth already belongs to Him, He puts the Israelites (and us) in a difficult position. After all, what do you give the God who has everything? Yes, we can give God our time, talents and money even though all these things are already His, and God does not rebuke us for that. But He does rebuke Israel (and us) for giving those things to Him while failing to give Him what He really wants.

14

What can we give the God who has everything? Unlike my dear grandparents, who never gave me a clue what they wanted, God spells out very clearly the two gifts He desires from His people: "Make thanksgiving your sacrifice to God," He says, and "Call on Me in the day of trouble, [and] I will deliver you . . ." The two gifts God wants most from us are our thanksgiving and our prayers.

"Give thanks in all circumstances," (1 Thessalonians 5:18) is a theme which runs through the entire Bible. Give thanks always — in triumph and tragedy, through laughter and tears and in every situation you face in life, give thanks. Let your sense of thanksgiving run so deep in the very core of your being that this is the offering you are continually making to the Lord.

Give thanks even when you aren't sure what you are giving thanks for! That's what a group of commuters on a London train did one day. It seems that the 5 p.m. train from London out to the western suburbs was supposed to take just half an hour, but it ran late every evening, taking up to an hour, even an hour and a half sometimes. The trip was even slower on Fridays, when everyone was especially eager to get home and start their weekend.

One Friday evening, the train made it out to the last suburban stop in just 20 minutes. Better than being on time, it was actually early! The passengers stepped off the train and surged toward the conductor to thank him. "Don't thank me," the conductor said, "I just learned how to stop this thing five minutes ago!"

Give thanks always, no matter what you are going through at the moment. Make thanksgiving the basic attitude which infuses your life at all times and in every situation.

Many of us would admit that it would be nice to live that way, but we would quickly add that it is hard to always feel thankful. "I'd feel more thankful if I could," we say, "but I'm too busy! I've got such a crazy schedule, frantically running around between work and home and volunteer meetings and everything else I have to do that I just haven't got time to be very thankful!"

Others would say, "I'd be more thankful if I didn't have so much to worry about in these trying times. I'm looking at a possible layoff next month, my taxes and insurance are going up, and I can hardly pay the bills I've got now!" Or, "I'm looking at a health problem or a nursing home decision just down the road. It's hard to feel thankful in the midst of all this uncertainty!"

Despite all this, do you think there is a way to develop that sense of thanksgiving which stays within you no matter what? Perhaps I can best begin by telling you two ways not to do it!

First, there's the old cliche, "Count your many blessings." When you're feeling down or troubled, stop for a minute and count your blessings. Then you'll remember what you can be thankful for.

The problem with this is that Christian thanksgiving does not depend on blessings. Indeed, Christian thanksgiving grows in power and strength when our blessings seem few and far between. What did Jesus do on the night He was betrayed? He celebrated what we now call the Eucharist, a word which comes from the Latin word for "thanksgiving." "And when He had given thanks for [the bread], He broke it and said, 'Take this bread and eat ...'" Thanksgiving is woven into the very heart of our worship at the Lord's table because thanksgiving was at the very heart of our Lord's faith.

What did the Pilgrims do after landing on these shores? They had suffered terribly during their persecution in the Old World and their voyage to the New World. Half of their small company had already died. In the midst of all this anguish and death, they did the only logical thing: they gathered with their new native neighbors for a thanksgiving meal! Real Christian thanksgiving does not depend one iota on having a lot of blessings to count.

The other way not to feel more thankful is found in another popular cliche: compare yourself to other people whose situations are worse than your own. We say to someone who is mourning the death of his mother, "Well, don't feel so bad, I just read in the newspaper about a man who lost his whole family in a car accident!" We say to someone who just had her hours cut back at work, "Well, consider yourself lucky: there are millions of people in Africa who have no home and are dying of starvation!"

Again, does this sound very Christian to you? If we hear of someone whose situation is so much harder or poorer than our own, isn't the Christian response to go and help that person or attack that injustice, rather than be thankful that we are not suffering as badly as they are? We don't reflect on the miseries or misfortunes of others in order to feel better about ourselves.

In order to be thankful all the time, we must begin by remembering to whom we are thankful. That is what Harriet Martineau needed to learn, a 19th century English writer who was a well-known atheist. It is said that she was walking with her friend one autumn day, taking in the glorious fall colors splashed around her, and suddenly she exclaimed, "Oh, I am so thankful!" Her friend turned to her and said, "Thankful to whom, my dear?"

If we always have someone to be thankful to, we always have a reason to be thankful, and the One we always have to be thankful to is God. We can simply be thankful that God is God, who abides forever and does not come and go like autumn colors on a tree. This knowledge and remembrance of the constancy of God is the foundation of our gratitude. It puts within us a profound sense of thanksgiving which comforts and sustains us no matter how hard the blustery winds of life's storms may blow or toss us to and fro.

This same God who abides is always there for us in times of need. Indeed, our text tells us that this is precisely what God is asking for — it is the second gift He wants from us.

God wants our prayers. "Call on Me in the day of trouble," He says in our text; "I will deliver you and you will glorify Me." Sometimes God comes to us just as we begin to fall into despair with an inner sense that He is there. Sometimes God sends His love through other people, people who will stand by us unconditionally and be there for us through thick and

17

thin. In one way or another, God says we may call on Him to deliver us in our time of trouble. This is a source of great spiritual security and another reason to live our lives each day with an attitude of gratitude.

What other reasons do we have for being grateful to God? We may be grateful for the salvation He has given us in His Son, Jesus Christ, for the promises we received with His resurrection, for the assurance of forgiveness and everlasting life. When we look at our condition from the standpoint of eternity, doesn't it put our present problems in their proper perspective, and isn't this another source of continual thanksgiving which the world can neither give nor take away?

We can be thankful that God has put His Holy Spirit within us, allowing us to love and serve. We can be grateful for the gift of conscience, that we may be moved to the struggle for God's justice and peace. All of these divine gifts make us not mere accidents of chemistry or biology, insignificant specks of dust destined for oblivion, but nothing less than children of the Lord God Almighty, and we are profoundly grateful for that as well.

Yes, there is a way to be thankful through all the joys and sorrows of life. It begins by remembering our relationship to God and remembering in faith who we are as recipients of God's many gifts — spiritual gifts which do not depend on transient blessings or the comparative sufferings of others or the ebb and flow of worldly fortunes.

Even when the world and everyone in it seems to turn against us, we may be thankful. Even when our life's struggles seem in vain and discouragement casts its lengthening shadow across our souls, we may be thankful. Even when we feel alone and unappreciated, wondering where we will find the good cheer and grace to go on giving, we may be thankful. We may continue to offer God our gifts of thanksgiving, because there remains a spiritual anchor within which holds us steady and reminds us of His love.

Surely, we help ourselves and make ourselves happier if we offer thanksgiving for all things, even adversity. More importantly, we make God happy as well, since He has made it abundantly clear that prayers and thanksgiving are the gifts He wants from us. He who has the whole world in His hands has been gracious enough to tell us what we may give to the God who has everything. Amen.

## Pastoral Prayer

**O Good and Gracious God, who continually holds us in the loving arms of Your divine concern, we praise You today for all the gifts You so freely bestow upon us — spiritual gifts which can never be counted or repaid. We praise You for the gifts of love and life, for visions of faith and hope, for stirrings of compassion and charity, for the promises and assurances which will bless us for eternity. We who sometimes feel so forlorn and battered about are heartened by your dependable presence, which gives us so much and asks only in return that we be thankful enough to love You daily and love our neighbor as ourselves. Help us, dear God, to make gratitude the wellspring from which our lives of love and faith may freely flow. In Jesus' name, we pray. Amen.**

# You Are All That
# Matters To God

**Psalm 50:7-12**
**"I know all the birds of the air, and all that moves
in the field is mine."** **(v. 11)**

Imagine you had 35 brothers and sisters! Think of it ...
36 children in the family, including yourself, all living in one
house! What do you think that would be like? How do you
think a family like that would manage? *(Let them answer.)*

I imagine they would have to take turns eating, since it
would be hard to find a table and a dining room big enough
for 36 kids and two parents. I imagine everyone would have
bunk beds and there would be at least six children in every
room. They would probably have to vote every night on which
television shows to watch, since no family would have 36 television sets in one house! And think of what it would be like
trying to get 36 kids bathed and fed and ready to go some-
where. To get everyone cleaned up and ready for school on
Monday morning, for example, they would have to start the
baths on Saturday afternoon!

If you are in a family that big, you might also wonder how
much attention your parents could really give to you or any
other child in particular. You might think your own problems
and needs would get overlooked because your parents would
have so many other children to worry about. I have three small
children myself, and I know that every time I give time to one
of them, the other two want me to do something with them
also. Three children constantly competing for one parent's time

— imagine how hard it would be to get attention in a house with 36 children!

We might think this would be an even bigger problem with God. After all, God has so much more to worry about than just one family. He has to look after all the children and all the grown-ups all over the world. Then he also has to be concerned about all the animals, fish, bugs, plants, trees and everything else that moves and grows in the world. And let's not forget the rest of the universe, all the other planets and stars and comets and black holes and anything else that might be out there. When we think of things in this way, we might easily feel that God is just too busy to pay attention to what's going on with you or me.

The Bible says God isn't like that. God cares so much about His world that He knows everything there is to know about it — He even knows all the birds that fly in the air! No bird, no plant, no animal is too small or too unimportant for God's concern; He knows what is going on with each and every one of His creatures.

Jesus talked about all this one day and made it more plain. He told a group of people: if God cares this much for each bird of the air and flower of the field, how much more does God care about you? (c.f. Matthew 6:26-30) Are not boys and girls who think and talk and laugh and cry all the more important to God?

What the Bible tells us is that we need never fear that God is too big or too busy to be bothered with us — that's something important to be thankful for, isn't it! Yes, it may seem that God has a lot of people and things to keep in mind, but God is so great that He can do it with ease. The minute we pray to Him, the moment we feel lost and need Him, God stops everything, and like the loving parent He is, God pays attention to us as if we are all that matter in the world. Amen.

# Hector's Case
# Against Christmas

**Luke 1:26-38**
**"In the sixth month, the angel Gabriel was sent by**
**God to a town in Galilee named Nazareth."**
**(v. 26)**

I am going to begin the Advent season this year by telling you a part of the Christmas story which is unknown to most people because it was left out of the modern Bible. Of course, ministers have known about this for many years, but we have kept it secret because we didn't want to shake anyone's faith. But in this age of full and complete disclosure, I have finally decided to break with my fellow clergy's conspiracy of silence and tell you this neglected part of the Christmas story.

The truth which has been hidden from you until now is that not everyone was happy with God's decision to send His Son into the world. Certainly, the angel Gabriel was happy he was chosen to give Mary the word, since everyone likes being the bearer of good news, and our text tells us that after a moment of doubt and reluctance, Mary was thrilled to be so favored by God among women. But it is quite wrong to look solely at the characters in scripture and infer that everyone was happy about the first Christmas.

You see, there was another angel who was quite upset that God would do this, who thought it was a terrible idea to let Jesus be born in Bethlehem or anywhere else for that matter. This is the angel our modern Bible doesn't tell you about. His name was Hector.

22

Hector was a distant cousin of Gabriel's on his mother's side, and he had always been known as something of a pessimist and cynic. His natural instinct was to expect the worst in every person and every situation. He lived by the motto, "Never give suckers an even break because they will probably take advantage of you later." Hector was the kind of angel that after you shook hands with him, he would count his fingers to make sure you hadn't taken one.

At any rate, our story begins the day after Jesus' birth. Gabriel was sitting on a cloud high above the earth, basking in the afterglow of Christmas. He was remembering the joy on Mary's face when her labor was done. He was recalling with a warm smile the beautiful star and the simple faith of those who saw the baby that night. The choir of angels which sang to the shepherds in the field had never sounded better. ("Those extra rehearsals really paid off," Gabriel thought to himself.) God was in His heaven, Jesus Christ was born, Gabriel's suitcase was unpacked after his journey to earth, and all seemed right with the world.

Along came Hector. "Can we talk?" he asked. Gabriel wasn't thrilled about it since Hector's reputation for pessimism had made other angels shun him, even at family reunions, but being the angel he was, Gabriel agreed to talk with his distant cousin, Hector.

"I don't like to quarrel with God's decisions," Hector began, "but that was a real bad move, sending His only begotten Son to earth. It was the worst thing God could have done."

"You know," Gabriel said, "I thought that even you would appreciate what has just happened. What is there to quarrel with? How could anyone possibly make an argument against Christmas?"

"It was a wasted gesture on God's part," Hector began. "For one thing, people are too busy to notice Jesus or hear His message. What do you think people really care about anyway? Look at the way they live — do they really care about spiritual gifts like love or faith, or long-term blessings like salvation and eternal life? They can hardly think past today!

Look at them running around in a vain frenzy like ants on an ant hill, overscheduled and unfulfilled, clutching and grasping and cramming every waking moment with something terribly important to do.''

The two angels sat for a few minutes in pensive silence as Hector's harsh words sank in. Suddenly a picture came into view from the earth below — it was a family at home as the dinner hour approached. Mother and father had just come home from work and were trying to rush dinner on the table because Junior had to leave in 10 minutes for his triangle lesson. Older sister was home from her beginner's yodeling class but couldn't come to the table because her favorite game show was on television. What a family scene this was — the sound of screaming contestants blaring from the television, Junior gulping down his food and bolting out the door while mother and father sit there in numbed silence, their heads resting in their hands, too exhausted to talk or enjoy the meal.

"Do you see what I mean?" asked Hector. "If people can't even appreciate the gift of family life which is right before their eyes, how will they appreciate the gift of eternal life, which they will have to see through the eyes of faith?"

Gabriel didn't answer, so Hector continued. "Even if people do re-order their lives and pay more attention to what is really important," he said, "they won't believe the truth about Jesus anyway. Do you think the world will believe that a homeless child born of a teenaged girl in a dusty little town like Bethlehem is really the Son of God? This is a world where appearances are everything, Gabriel, and where all that matters are those things which can be consumed, acquired or exploited in the here and now."

Suddenly, Gabriel perked up. "That's where you are wrong," he said, "I sent out a press release yesterday to all the major news outlets announcing the birth of God's Son, so it will surely be a front page headline. In fact, today's newspapers are due to come out at any minute — let's see what they say."

24

The clouds parted again, and the two angels scanned the newspapers. There on the front page of the *Roman Empire News* was the picture of a spectacular chariot accident in downtown Athens. Next to that was a description of a debutante party for the rich and famous in Pompeii. This was followed by an editorial denouncing innkeepers who were raising their prices at a time when people were required to travel to distant villages to pay Caesar's tax.

Inside the paper were all the commodity prices, the latest odds on the Colosseum games, fashion tips and the weather report . . . everything except a story on the birth of God's Son! To be fair, there was a small article on the back page of the *Bethlehem Banner,* right beneath the horoscopes. The headline read, "Local Girl Claims Virgin Birth," but the article went on to say: "Authorities believe that given the public backlash against the current epidemic of teenaged pregnancies, this is a case of a young girl trying to explain herself to her parents and her boyfriend."

Satisfied by Gabriel's silence that his point had been made, Hector went on to his third argument against Christmas. "Besides the fact that people are too busy to notice Jesus and won't believe Him anyway, the plain truth is that the world is far too dangerous for Jesus to be sent in alone. Where are His bodyguards? Where are His weapons? How can we guarantee His safety? Do you know what happens to people who try to do good in this world, or who offend the powers that be? They get assassinated! The authorities put them away! This world is far too dangerous for a man like Jesus," Hector said. "They'll never let Him die a natural death."

Suddenly, another earthly picture came into view, this time a family gathering in Israel. The year is 4 B.C. and an extended family is celebrating the impending birth of a child. People are having a wonderful time, dancing and singing, catching up with aunts, uncles and cousins they haven't seen in years.

"Do you see that?" asked Gabriel. "There is also some love and joy to be found in this world; it isn't all just violence and danger, betrayal and death. The two angels listen as the

220494

expectant father stops the dancing to make a toast. "I thank God for this child who is to come," he says. "If it is a girl, my wife will name her. If it is a boy, I will name him Judas."

Hector smiled triumphantly at the name of Judas. "That clinches it!" he cried. "I believe I have made my case against Christmas." By now, even Gabriel was wondering if Hector wasn't right. "Maybe God did make a mistake in sending Jesus to an unbelieving world which was too busy and too dangerous to receive Him," he said to himself.

At that very moment, another picture came in through the parted clouds. A father was tucking his little girl into bed. "I'm scared in the dark, Daddy," she said. "Please come and sit beside me until I fall asleep." "But God is there with you, even in the dark," the father said gently. "I know that Daddy, but I want someone beside me with skin on."

"Did you hear that?" asked Gabriel. "I will grant you everything you have said about the world. I will grant you that Jesus will not be accepted in the world He has come to save. But that little girl just told us why God has done this. People are afraid of the dark ... afraid of the dark sin within them and the dark death beyond them. People need to know they aren't alone in the night, Hector. They need a God beside them with skin on."

Hector still wasn't quite clear on the concept. "Don't you see?" said Gabriel. "The heart of what ails people is their sense of separation from God. They can't live as morally and courageously as they want to live because they feel hopelessly cut off from God's goodness and light. But now God has removed all distance between Himself and His people. Now God has put skin on and drawn near to people who could not draw near to Him, and brought light to people who could not see past the darkness. God has made Himself available to people in the form they can most easily understand — the form of their own flesh and blood."

Suddenly, time flashed forward to the present year, and the two angels saw a group of people gathered in a church. It wasn't just any church; it was our own church right here in _____ on the first Sunday in Advent, and people were celebrating communion.

They were remembering Jesus as He had told them to remember Him: in the bread and cup. They were giving thanks that Jesus had come to them as God with skin on, bringing eternity down from the heavens and putting it within their grasp. Yes, they were still too busy and too unbelieving, and yes, the world was still too dangerous a place for love to live unharmed, but there was a peace and a joy within these people anyway. As they listened to the familiar words of Jesus and shared His fellowship in that sacred meal, they knew they were receiving an inner assurance and a lasting hope which the world can test but never destroy.

Hector was so impressed by what he saw that he changed his mind about Christmas. In fact, his whole attitude changed, to the point where he wasn't shunned any more at family reunions. So, as you celebrate communion today, remember the faith Hector saw which made him change his mind. Let your spirits receive a special lift on this first Sunday in Advent as you celebrate the light and the love which are coming into the world. Be especially grateful as you receive the bread and cup today. After all, it could well be that a couple of angels are watching. Amen.

### Pastoral Prayer

**Most gracious and generous God, who gave up what is most dear to You for our good and the good of the world, we thank You today for this season of Advent, a season of expectation and hope. Help us to remain focused, not on the commercial noise around us, but on the growing joy within us. Help us to be grateful that You loved the world so much as to come to us Yourself, in the form of our own flesh and blood, that a God with skin on could remain next to us when we stand fearful before the night. Inspire us by this gift to give as well to others, that we may touch others with tangible comfort and help in their time of need. In Jesus' name, we pray. Amen.**

# Wondering How God Does Things

**Luke 1:26-38**
**"Nothing will be impossible with God."**

**(v. 37)**

Do you ever wonder how God does things? You may remember that we talked last week about how many people and animals and other things God has to pay attention to, so that's a good place to start. How does God keep track of so many different things? If everyone in the world is praying to God all at the same time, each in their own language and each with their own need, how does God hear everyone? I don't know! I can only wonder how God does things like that.

Then there are other questions we might ask about God. How did God get just two of every kind of animal to go on Noah's ark and why did He include mosquitoes? How does God put the yoke of an egg inside a shell? How did God think of such a wild variety of plants and flowers, with all their different colors, sizes and shapes, and how did God teach the animals what they know about surviving and having young and taking care of themselves? Come to think of it, how could God be big enough to make this universe we live in, and where do you and I come from?

What are some of the things you wonder about? *(Let them answer.)* You see? There is no end to the questions we could ask and the mysteries we could explore as we wonder about how God does things.

We see this same kind of wonder in the Christmas story, when the angel Gabriel comes to visit Mary and tells her she is going to be the mother of God's Son. Mary can't understand it. "How can this be?" she says, "How can I possibly have a baby?" The angel Gabriel didn't explain it to her; all he said was, "The Holy Spirit will come to you," and "Nothing will be impossible with God." Mary, too, was left to wonder about how God does things.

You children are always asking questions because you want to understand what things are and how they work. Sometimes you ask us questions we can answer, like why the sky is blue, or how far it is from home plate to first base on a big league baseball diamond. But when you ask us questions about God, we can't always be sure what to say. If you ask whether God loves us, we can tell you for certain that He does; God loves and cares for all His children. But other questions you might ask have no answer, and we can only say that we don't know. This is how it should be, because after all, if we knew everything there is to know about God, if we had all the answers about God, God wouldn't be God! God wouldn't be the Almighty Wonder that He is, far beyond even our biggest thoughts and anything we can imagine.

Just like Mary when the angel came to visit her, there will be some things we will never understand about God, but also like Mary, we should know that this is all right. Don't be afraid to let God be a mystery. Don't think you need to have God all figured out "from A to Z" in order to believe in Him. In fact, one of the best things to be said about having faith in an awesome God like ours is that sometimes it's okay just to marvel at Him, and to wonder about how He does things. Amen.

# The Ultimate Christmas Gift

**Psalm 85:8-13; Ephesians 2:11-22**
**"The Lord will speak ... to His people."**
**(Psalm 85:8)**

As we consider the wide variety of gifts we might receive this Christmas, we could probably place those gifts in one of several categories.

First and least importantly, there are those entirely frivolous items which we do not need and never intend to use. How many of us, for example, have received things like automatic toothpick dispensers or electric yarn untanglers which now sit forgotten on some closet shelf collecting dust? Then again, there is no accounting for taste. Years ago, I received a necktie which looked exactly like a piece of bacon, complete with brown stripes to represent the meat and yellow stripes to represent the fat. I am certain the person who gave it to me never intended I wear it, but I liked that "bacon tie" and wore it for several years, until one day an embarrassed girlfriend yanked it off my neck and ritualistically burned it, declaring it utterly "gross," disgusting and unfit for human haberdashery.

Then there are the more serious gifts we appreciate receiving but could easily have acquired for ourselves: a best-selling book we have always wanted to read, for example, or a nice necktie that doesn't look like a piece of bacon. Ranked even higher than that on our hierarchy of gifts might be those things we want or need but could not have bought ourselves, such as a teenager receiving a new car from her parents, or a retired couple receiving a trip around the world from their children.

Finally, there are those Christmas gifts others give us which cannot be purchased in any store. A long-estranged family member visits for the holidays and buries the hatchet. A much-dreaded medical test comes back on the day before Christmas, and it is "negative." All of your children and grandchildren come home for Christmas, making it the first time everyone has been together in 15 years. Surely, these emotional gifts mean more than all the material gifts piled up under the tree, and we might well think they are the highest category of gift we can receive at Christmas.

But what about an even greater, more glorious gift than that? Imagine receiving the ultimate Christmas gift, a gift so awesome and wondrous that even as you hold it in your hands, you do not believe it is yours? You tell other people about this gift and they do not believe you either, because it is a gift which cannot be purchased for any price or obtained by even the most strenuous of human effort. It is a gift so far removed from our experience, so far beyond our grasp and abilities that we have not even dared to dream we might some day receive it.

Yet receive this gift we did on a silent, holy night so long ago in Bethlehem. It was announced by a choir of angels who came upon the midnight clear. "Glory to God in the highest," the angels sang, "and on earth, peace, goodwill among all people." (Luke 2:14) This was God's clear message to humankind and God's explicit intention for us with the birth of His Son, spelled out in heavenly harmonies for all the world to hear.

We do not understand this because we do not see it in the world around us, but the ultimate Christmas gift is peace! Not just peace of mind or eternal peace beyond the grave, but peace and goodwill in this world, in the "here and now!" This is so basic to the meaning of Advent that we cannot neglect it without trivializing the season. Beyond the gifts and family reunions we like to think about, and even beyond the birth of the baby Jesus, no season of Advent worship can be complete without at least one serious attempt to wrestle with the problem and promise of peace.

31

Understand that I am not talking today about any particular crisis or hot spot in the world which may command our attention at the moment. There are wars and rumors of wars all around us, while words like aggression and national interest, freedom and tyranny are tossed about in every part of the world with self-serving regularity. So the news headlines remind us daily.

As dangerous and serious as these situations are (and some are much closer to home than we realize), to the Christian they are still symptoms of a deeper rebellion and more profound spiritual disorder. We say even in this violent, war-torn world that Advent brings the gift of peace on earth, but only in a biblical sense can we know what this gift means and how it is realized in the world.

When most people speak of peace, they mean the absence of war, and even the Bible occasionally uses the word in that sense. Two kings sign a treaty and so they make peace. (e.g. 1 Kings 5:12) But far more common in scripture is the more positive view of peace as *shalom,* a wholistic condition of universal compatibility and prosperity, unity and abundance. More than the mere absence of war, *shalom* is a harmonious state of being which is shared by all, to the point where war is not only impossible but even unthinkable.

When most people speak of peace, they think of it as something to be won or created through treaties, alliances and so on. The Bible says quite the opposite: that all peace comes from God and comes only as a gift from God. "God will speak to His people," our text from Psalms says, and God has, indeed, spoken peace to us consistently through the ages, teaching us what Jesus called "the things that make for peace." (Luke 19:42)

After all these years, are "the things that make for peace" still a mystery to us? "Do justice, love mercy and walk humbly with your God." (Micah 6:8) Do not "oppress the poor" (Amos 4:1) or "answer roughly the entreaties of the needy," (Proverbs 18:23) and do not let some acquire so much of God's earth for themselves that others are left without (cf. Isaiah 5:8), for this brings not peace and prosperity, but resentment and rebellion.

Jesus put it in words so simple they have never been tried! Let people and nations make friends of their enemies by treating others as they themselves would be treated. (cf. Luke 6:31) Let those who have much realize their common destiny with those who have little. Let world leaders and treaty negotiators create a lasting peace by paying as much attention to their adversaries' needs and interests as they do their own. The biblical maxim, "Love your neighbor as yourself," is political as well as personal wisdom, for whether it be in a nearby inner city or a faraway Third World village, in the long run, there can be peace for no one without justice for everyone.

Then, says our Psalm, "steadfast love and faithfulness shall meet." Valleys of injustice and squalid deprivation shall be lifted up, and mountains of excess and inequity shall be made low. The uneven ground which selfish greed has fashioned shall become level and the rough places of disadvantage shall become smooth. (cf. Isaiah 40:4) Then, says our Psalm, "faithfulness shall spring up from the ground and righteousness look down from the sky," and the gift of God's peace "shall dwell in the land."

The prophet Jeremiah spoke for all God's faithful in every age when he railed against those who "Cry 'peace, peace' when there is no peace." (6:14) He railed against those who are stifled in the straitjacket of the status quo, believing that the bellicosity which led to war in the past will somehow lead to peace in the future. God alone gives peace, and He uproots and rearranges our moral geography in order to do it. Only a spiritual revolution, a moral about face, a righteousness born of obedience to God's Word can make us ready to receive God's precious gift of peace.

Of course, human history is the tragic story of our turning to ourselves and not to God for the peace we so ardently need and seek. Indeed, we have yearned so desperately but so misguidedly for peace through the years that we have vainly tried to create it in many different ways.

33

Some have tried peace through conquest and have actually managed to eliminate war for a time, but festering resentments among those who are conquered only lead to war and rebellion again.

Some have tried peace through strength and intimidation, hoping that peace will come from the threat of war, but the same human pride which causes one side to issue the threat usually causes the other side to resist the threat, leaving both sides locked arm in arm and sliding inexorably down a slippery slope into moral and then economic bankruptcy, or even into war itself.

Some have tried peace through appeasement, hoping to delay war by placating an enemy, and some have tried peace through poverty, hoping to avoid war by ridding themselves of anything an enemy might want. Still others have tried using overwhelming force, hoping to gain peace by ending war quickly, but when they inevitably inflict mass destruction upon innocent civilians as well as enemy soldiers, they find that while they have won the war, they have lost the values they were fighting to defend in the first place. All of these and many other approaches have filled the sad pages of human history, and none has produced peace on any scale for any length of time.[1]

God saw and knew all this down through the years, through bloody century after bloody century, until finally, as the prophets had promised He would, God did a new thing. (Isaiah 43:18) Rather than leaving peace as a philosophy or a strategy, or even a standard of righteousness which humanity in history has never attained, God made peace a person. He sent us His only Son, who is our "Prince of Peace." (Isaiah 9:6) "God spoke peace," and the Word God spoke "became flesh and lived among us." (John 1:14)

Peace became a person. "For He is our peace," declares Paul of Jesus Christ in our text from Ephesians. In His flesh, Christ has broken down the barriers of hostility between us, making peace between all people, and peace between all people and God. "Before we had no hope" because we were "without God in the world," Paul says, but now God is in the world in the person of Jesus Christ, and because He is, we now have hope. We now have peace.

However, we will not receive this peace which God has given us until we understand that it must first be realized at a profoundly spiritual level before it can be realized corporally in our homes, our communities or the world. There is simply no other way.

Peace cannot be imposed from the "top down," as myriad emperors, kings, dictators and presidents have amply demonstrated throughout the annals of recorded history. Nor can peace be imposed from the "bottom up," because revolutions and rebellions, even when motivated by the desire to create justice, inevitably replace one form of violence with another. No, peace cannot come from the "top down" or the "bottom up" — it can only come from the "inside out." It must begin in the human heart and find expression in lives which are subordinated to the spirit of the person who is our peace, the baby who is born in Bethlehem.

Thus, the path to peace lies in emulating the Man that baby became. In personal and in political terms, peace is no longer an abstract idea but an embodied ideal which is available to everyone because it is found in the love, forgiveness, service and sacrifice which are the essence of Christian spirituality. We look in vain to our own devices and are misled by secular wisdoms; true peace has come to us at last in the person of Jesus Christ.[2]

Is this not what God has done by sending His own Son to our hostile, warring world? So long as Christ lives in our midst, there is peace in Him who is our peace. So long as He lives among us, He unites in love all who are living for Him. He is *shalom* in the world — God's ultimate Christmas gift which fills our hearts this Advent season and which someday shall fill the earth. Today, we rejoice in His coming and seek to live in His ways, for in Him, our God has spoken, and the word God has spoken is peace. Amen.

## Pastoral Prayer

O Holy and Righteous God, who spoke first the Word of creation and then the Word of peace, we pray today that all the empty and aching corners of our hearts will be filled with the peace of Christ which passes all understanding. Let His peace within us govern our relationships with family and friends, that we may be as patient and forbearing with our loved ones as we truly want to be. Let Christ's peace within lift us above the pressures and traumas we face, that we may be more than conquerors through him who loves us, living gracefully and victoriously through all of life's changing circumstances. And let His peace within us remove all fear as we face the uncertainties of life, even the greater uncertainty of death, that we may be lifted on wings of faith above every doubt, certain in our hearts that the jet streams which carry us onward are leading us to Your promise.

O Gracious God, who speaks the Advent word of peace on earth and goodwill to all people, we pray as well that all the world shall be filled with the peace of this child whose birth we await in Bethlehem. Let rulers of nations everywhere join in sweet anthems of peace, and let the rough words of war pass from their lips no more. Make all of us instruments of Your peace, O God, sowing harmony and understanding where there is enmity and hatred, sowing justice and charity where there is deprivation and want, being peacemakers in the manner and spirit of our Savior, whose word is peace and who is our peace, even Jesus Christ, our Lord. Amen.

---

[1]One other significant approach to peace was the attempt to limit the way wars were conducted. Building upon ideas which originated in classical

philosophy, Augustine and others in the medieval church proscribed rules for initiating and conducting a "just war" — the war must be fought for a just cause, the war must be declared by a legitimate authority, civilians are not to be attacked, the force used must be proportionate to the need, and so on. The hope was that restraint in war would cause less hardship and breed less resentment, thereby making peace more likely once the war was over.

Most historians agree that the American Civil War marked the end of the limited or just war era. As our Civil War began, civilian families streamed out of Washington, D.C. to enjoy picnics on the surrounding hillsides while watching the Battle of Bull Run. By the time the Civil War ended, General Sherman was scorching the earth on his way to Atlanta, and the idea of a limited war which restricted the use of force and spared civilians was gone forever.

Today, of course, modern technology has removed all restraints from the conduct of war. Because nations at war feel obliged to win the war as quickly as possible, they use (even non-nuclear) weapons of mass destruction which blur all distinctions between civilian and military casualties — a means of conducting war which has been "universally condemned since the Dark Ages." (Fred Ikle)

[2] I am aware that the Christian realism of Reinhold Niebuhr and others insists that individuals are far more able to embody ideals like love, justice and peace than are societies and nations. Niebuhr expounded this thesis most persuasively in his classic work, *Moral Man and Immoral Society*. Nevertheless, while principles of peace can readily be applied in personal living, they can also be translated into political terms and approximated on a social scale. Earlier in this sermon, for example, mention was made of creating a lasting peace by negotiating with the adversary's interests in mind as much as one's own. Political theorists relate such an approach to what they call "double loop learning;" it represents a secularized approximation of a Christian principle. (See, for example, Stanley Harakas, "The N.C.C.B. Pastoral Letter, The Challenge of Peace: An Eastern Orthodox Response," in *Peace in a Nuclear Age*, Charles Reid, ed., Catholic University of America Press, Washington, D.C., 1986, pp. 268-272.)

37

# Jesus Brings
# People Together

**Ephesians 2:11-22**
**"For He is our peace; in His flesh He has made both
groups one and has broken down the dividing wall
of hostility between us."** **(v. 14)**

Today I want you to divide yourselves into separate groups,
and I am going to divide you by the color of your eyes. Who
has blue eyes? Sit over here. Who has brown eyes? Sit over
there. Who has green eyes? You sit here.

Now suppose I told you that from this moment on, you
must not like anyone who isn't in your group. If you have
brown eyes, you aren't supposed to like anyone with blue eyes.
If you have green eyes, you must hate everyone with brown
eyes, and so on. They are different from you. They're bad.
You can't trust them, and they are not as nice as you.

Does that make any sense to you? Should we like some
people because their eyes are the same color as ours, and not
like other people because their eyes are a different color?

You probably know that even children have many ways
of dividing themselves into groups of friends and enemies. They
call their own group good and other groups bad, and then they
find reasons to hate and hurt each other. This is a sin we call
prejudice.

Sometimes you see it in school, particularly during recess.
In elementary school, boys and girls may be against each other
and stand around the playground making fun of each other.

Or maybe there is a new kid in school, and a group of old friends makes him feel unwelcome.

Of course, children have learned this from grown-ups, who have been putting up dividing walls between themselves forever. If it isn't the color of peoples' eyes, it's the color of their skin that divides them. People hate each other just because their skin is a different color. Or because they practice a different religion, come from a different country, speak a different language or have a different point of view about important questions.

In Jesus' day, the grown-ups built an actual dividing wall inside the temple in Jerusalem. One group of people were told to stay on one side of the wall, and the other group of people had to stay on the other side of the wall. Imagine what that was like! Imagine us having a high wall running right down the middle of our church, with blue-eyed people worshiping God on one side and brown-eyed people worshiping God on the other side?

The Bible says that with the coming of Jesus, the walls which divide people no longer exist. "Jesus is our peace," the Bible says: "He has made both groups into one and has broken down the dividing wall [of] hostility between us." We don't often think of this when we think about Christmas, what with all the fun we have with presents, pageants and Christmas carols, but Jesus' birth also means that a new kind of peace is born. A baby is coming who makes all people one. Blue eyes and green eyes, white skin and black skin, yellow, brown and red skin ... all people can love each other since God loves all people through Him. Jesus brings people together, which is all the more reason to be joyful in this beautiful and loving Advent season. Amen.

# When Is The Baby Coming?

**Luke 2:1-7**
**"While they were there, the time came for her to deliver her child."** **(v. 6)**

"When is the baby coming?" Every expectant parent who ever lived has asked that question, but the answer is always the same. Babies come when they feel like coming! Sometimes they come early, as if they can't wait to get out on their own. Sometimes they come late, as if they had heard the evening news too many times while lying in their mother's womb and decided they are better off where they are. Modern medicine confidently gives the parents what it calls a "due date," but that is about as pretentious as meteorologists making promises for the weather. For all our sophisticated tests and predictions, babies never come at the precise time and place of the parents' (or the doctor's) choosing.

I have heard stories about babies being born in hospital elevators or in the back seats of cars which were racing to the hospital. Clearly, the mothers of those children would not have chosen those times and places for giving birth. Certainly, Mary was no different, and I imagine she would have preferred to be in Nazareth, surrounded by the comforts of home and the support of her family when Jesus was born. But the baby Jesus did not come while Mary was in Nazareth. He came while she found herself in a rude animals' stable in Bethlehem.

"When is the baby coming?" Parents ask the question more urgently as the pregnancy enters its final months. The father asks anxiously, "Will the baby come in the middle of the night, or while I am at work?" The mother asks dejectedly, "Will this baby ever come?" Again, I imagine that question also crossed Mary's mind as she took that long, slow, agonizing journey along the bumpy road from Nazareth to Bethlehem, riding on the back of a donkey.

Parents have much to prepare before the baby arrives, and our text suggests what Mary did to get ready for the birth of Jesus. She must have gathered some swaddling cloths before she left home in order to wrap the baby, since we know she had them with her in the Bethlehem stable that night. She might also have packed some salt, since it was the custom in those days to rub the newborn baby with salt before putting on the wrapping cloths. Like good parents everywhere, Mary did what she could to be ready when the time came.

The Bible says that God was also busy preparing for the birth of His Son. First, He sent the angel Gabriel to speak with an old man named Zechariah, to prepare him and his aged wife, Elizabeth, for the birth of a son to be named John, who would grow up to baptize Jesus and announce His mission. (Luke 1:5ff) God also sent Gabriel to visit Mary, to give her the news which would make her blessed among women forever. (Luke 1:26ff) Then God caused Joseph to be visited in a dream, to convince Joseph to go through with his marriage to Mary and not divorce her quietly as he had planned. (Matthew 1:18ff) All of this had to be done and all of these people had to be involved before the baby Jesus could be born.

"When is the baby coming?" In their own way, today's parents still prepare for the coming of a child during the long months of pregnancy. Perhaps they buy a crib and some toys, and fix up the baby's room. If you are like my wife, you do all of that within 30 minutes after you've learned you are pregnant, and then you spend nine months buying every piece of clothing the child will need from birth through high school. If you are like me, you spend nine months wearing out the starter on your car by checking every 10 minutes to make sure it will start when the big moment arrives.

41

Of course, we don't stay that neurotic and compulsive forever. My mother-in-law raised nine children, and she jokingly observed one day that the manner of your preparation changes as you go along. "The first child gets everything," she said. "You lay out the baby's room, fill it with new clothes and make sure everything is ready months before that first child is born."

"You still prepare for the second child," she went on. "But you don't worry quite as much if the room isn't ready on time, and the clothes are now "hand-me-downs" instead of new. As the children keep coming, you prepare a little less each time. By the time you get to the fifth or sixth child," she said, "they are lucky if they get a name!"

I wonder if that is how some of us prepare for the coming of Jesus each year. Do we get more casual about the birth of this child as the Christmas seasons come and go? Does it all become routine, to the point where we are preparing for Jesus not as a first-born child, but as a fifth- or sixth-born child?

On the surface, it appears that the danger of doing this is very real. After all, what do we do to get ready for the birth of Jesus when Advent rolls around? We go into the attic or closet and pull out the same old Christmas boxes we have used for years. We put the same lights in the same windows every year. We put the same little creches or Santas in the same places we have always put them. We hang the same stockings on the same nails and put the tree in its familiar place, filling it with the familiar decorations and placing the familiar star on top.

There may be some value to all this tradition and continuity in material terms, and it probably gives comfort to us as adults to see our childhood stockings and ornaments still being used. But in spiritual terms, if we approach the birth of Jesus with that kind of sameness and predictability, the real meaning of Christmas will pass us by completely. After all, the point of Christmas is not only that Jesus Christ, the Son of God, was born among us, but also that our lives are profoundly changed because of His birth.

Think of how the birth of our own children changes our lives. For example, you give up forever the idea of having any extra money to save or spend. Phrases like "getting a good night's sleep" are permanently stricken from your vocabulary. Your formerly tidy house becomes a two-story toy box, and your formerly healthy body becomes a depository for every flu and virus that runs through the school system. You hear people talking about such things as peace and quiet and privacy and you wonder what foreign language they are speaking and what these strange words mean.

If I sound like a stressed-out parent, I should be fair and add that children bring other kinds of changes as well. Houses which once didn't know what they are missing are now filled with the sounds of child-like laughter and running feet. Words like joy and wonder acquire deeper meaning as we experience them anew through the eyes of children. Bonds of love grow more profound, connecting us to past and future generations, and allowing us to love our children unconditionally even as we are loved unconditionally by God.

Sometimes the coming of a child changes a whole community and not just an individual household, as we see in a marvelous short story by Bret Harte called *The Luck of Roaring Camp*. The story takes place in a rough and tumble mining town camp during the California Gold Rush. The entire town consists of rugged frontiersmen, miners, saloon keepers and one woman, who dies as her child is born.

Suddenly, a crude and coarse mining town called Roaring Camp is responsible for the care of a newborn baby, and remarkable changes begin to take place. Hardened frontiersmen become bath-givers and hard-bitten miners become nursemaids. Drinking and gambling are drastically reduced, and the men stop swearing when in the presence of the child. Old grudges are forgotten as former enemies unite in the common task of caring for a newborn baby.

The story doesn't say so, but it would be nice to think that the mine owners no longer required 12-hour shifts seven days a week, as was common in that era, but allowed the men more

43

time to nurture and care for the baby. What the story *does* say is that the mine in Roaring Camp which was thought to be stripped clean was suddenly producing gold again, so the baby was named "Luck."

Would not God be pleased to see something similar happen after the birth of a baby named Jesus, not just in a family or a town, but throughout the whole world? In a world full of Roaring Camps, where rough greed and rude strife rule the day, would not God be pleased to see this Baby's birth transform everyone everywhere into the loving and sharing people God means for us to be? For starters, would not God be pleased to see you and I approach Jesus' birth this year — not casually and predictably as if going through the motions of our 10th or 40th or 80th Christmas — but faithfully and spiritually, as if it were our very first one?

Our text says that the time came for Mary to be delivered. Indeed, that time of deliverance is fast approaching today. A baby sent from God is coming to change our lives and it is time to care for this child by acting in His name in service to others. It is time to reexamine the values we live by and conform our lifestyles to our convictions. It is time to rearrange our cluttered and confused priorities, and make a single commitment to Christ the center of all we do. It is time to refresh and restore our relationships with family and friends, and time to make straight our relationship with God.

When is the baby coming? The due date is December 25th, but as with all babies, we cannot be too sure. The actual day Christ is reborn within us may be earlier or later than that.

This baby will truly come to each one of us when we start caring more for His ways than our own, when we stop living in the old kingdom of this world which is passing away and start living in the new kingdom of God which is already coming. The day this baby truly comes to each one of us is the day we receive Him into our hearts and allow Him to change our lives forever. Then we shall know that the baby we have long been waiting for has come to us at last. Amen.

## Pastoral Prayer

Most Holy and Loving God, who is the faithful answer to every earnest prayer and the abiding hope of every steadfast heart, we ask You to move our spirits this Christmas season, that we may approach Jesus not as parents of a fifth- or sixth-born child, but as worshipers of the first-born Savior He is. Do not let us fall into spiritual ruts, even if we are surrounded by the familiar accoutrements of long-standing Christmas customs and conventions.

O God, let this be a season of spiritual rejuvenation, that our joy may be renewed and our strength restored, our faith reborn and our love reinspired. Be with those for whom this is a difficult season, and help them approach Christmas this year, not burdened by memories of Christmases past, but blessed by the feeling that they are experiencing this joyous and holy day for the very first time. In Jesus' name, we pray. Amen.

Children's Lesson For
Third Sunday In Advent

# Can You Go
# Home Again?

**Luke 2:1-7**

**"All went to their own towns to be registered. Joseph also went from the town of Nazareth in Galilee to Judea, to the city of David called Bethlehem, because he was descended from the house and family of David."** **(vv. 3-4)**

One day not too many years ago, I decided to go back to my old elementary school and see if my third-grade teacher was still there. It had been a long time since I had been back, and I thought it would be fun to see if she remembered me and if the school was as I remembered it to be.

Do you know what? Everything was different! My old teacher had retired, and someone else had taken her place. But that wasn't all that was different. They changed the desks. The desks were now so tiny! I remember being a third-grader and sitting very comfortably in normal-sized school desks, but these desks in my old classroom were so small that I couldn't even fit my knees under them! I remember the doorway used to be enormously high, towering way over my head; now it was just a regular doorway just barely taller than me. I walked down the hall to the water fountain, and a bubbler which used to be waist-high was now way down by the floor. I was so surprised at how the old place had changed that I went home and said to my wife, "Honey, they shrunk the school!"

Of course, the school hadn't changed at all; I was the one who was different! The desks, doorways and water fountains were the same size they had always been and were just fine for third-graders, but now that I was a fully-grown adult, they seemed very small to me.

I'll bet you have had similar experiences in your own lives. You may have had a favorite toy when you were a baby, for example, but now you can't play with that toy because you are older. You've changed, and you like different kinds of toys now.

We have an expression for this: we say, "You can't go home again." It means that as you get older and move on in life, you can't go back and find your old home, your old school, your old friends or toys exactly as you once knew them. You will have changed, the people, places and things you once knew will have changed, and nothing will be quite as you remembered it in your younger years.

We see this in the Christmas story, when Joseph and Mary traveled to Bethlehem, where their ancestors had lived. They went because a ruler named Caesar had ordered everyone to go back to their family's hometown to pay a tax. But when Joseph and Mary got there, they saw a very different Bethlehem than the one they remembered, since their small village was now so full of people that they couldn't even find a room to rent! They had to find a cave outside of town, which is where Mary gave birth to her baby, Jesus. Even Joseph and Mary couldn't go home again, because home was no longer the same little town of Bethlehem it once had been.

It may seem too bad that the people and places which mean so much to us in life change as the years go by. But there is one part of our life which never changes and to which we can always return. Of course, I am talking about God. The God we know is dependable and familiar. No matter what may happen as the years go by, you can always go to God for comfort, rest and help. You can trust Him to be the same good God He has always been, and because the goodness of our God is constant and forever, we need never feel lost or afraid when everything else changes in life. With God, we always know we have a safe place, a place to go home to again. Amen.

47

# Blessed Among Women

**1 Samuel 2:1-10; Luke 1:39-56**
**"And Elizabeth ... exclaimed with a loud cry, 'Blessed are you among women, and blessed is the fruit of your womb.' "** **(Luke 1:42)**

No one knows what she looked like. European artists have made her look European. African artists have made her look African. Native American artists have drawn her in their image, as have artists from South America, the Far East and nearly every other part of the world as well. In a sense, she has become the universal woman, adapted in every generation to every race and culture. One thing, however, artists everywhere have agreed upon: they have all depicted her as pious, thoughtful and serene.

"She," of course, is Mary, the mother of Jesus. When Elizabeth, pregnant with John the Baptist, first saw her, she exclaimed, "Blessed are you among women," and so it has been ever since. After Jesus Himself, no one has been more venerated, more honored or revered than this young girl from first century Israel. "Hail Mary, full of grace, the Lord is with thee ..." Hail the Blessed Virgin, the New Eve, Holy Mary, Mother of Mercy, Mother of God.

Before she became a statue in a church or an object of adoration in peoples' hearts, she was a woman and a person, and it is that part of Mary we want to recover this morning. What was she like? What kind of woman would be chosen by God to bear His Son, and what kind of woman would have the faith and grace to do it?

There are the usual qualities we traditionally think of. For example, we think of Mary as someone who was willing to take risks. She risked rejection by Joseph and even stoning by the other men in her village for being pregnant before she was married. She risked her own health and even her life by traveling to Bethlehem so close to term, and then giving birth unattended in a rude stable. She risked her life again by fleeing with Joseph to Egypt when a brutal dictator named Herod was seeking to kill her son.

Along with her courage, we traditionally think of Mary's humility, holding it up as a model of faithfulness in an age when humility is radically out of fashion. "Here am I, the servant of the Lord," she said; "let it be with me according to Your word." Here God was proposing not only an "unplanned pregnancy" but a dangerous one at that, and Mary did not refuse. She did not insist on her moral autonomy, her right to self-fulfillment or her freedom to control her body or her life. Instead, she yielded both to God, that she might be an instrument of His will.

"Let it be with me according to Your word." Mary allowed herself to be used and permitted her life to be changed forever in service to a higher good. Today that kind of self-subordination is condemned in many circles by women and men alike, who consider it "old-fashioned," "repressive" or "unliberated." It may be all of that and more in the eyes of the world, but Mary's spirit of self-giving obedience and humility surely remains beautiful in the eyes of God who wishes to see more of it in both men and women today.

Besides the courage and humility we usually associate with Mary, Luke's gospel tells us much more about her, because the opening chapters are written almost entirely from Mary's point of view.

Even as Luke first introduces us to Mary, as she encounters the angel Gabriel, we see that while Mary is faithful and obedient, she still has a mind of her own. Gabriel greets her by calling her "favored one," and immediately, the text says Mary is "perplexed." She "ponders what sort of greeting this might be." (1:28-29)

Perhaps she senses that to be favored by God is to have your life turned upside down. Perhaps she recalls her Old Testament scriptures, which amply demonstrate that people pay a price in this world for acting as servants of God. At any rate, we know that even before she was told about Jesus, Mary was wondering whether this calling from God was something she wanted to get involved with.

Then, when Gabriel tells her she will conceive a son, we see the practical and skeptical side of Mary. "How can this be," she asks, "since I am a virgin?" (Luke 1:34) At this point, she is thinking not of heavenly possibilities but biological realities.

Mary is also becoming part of a long tradition of people who argue and debate with God before accepting His will for their lives. Moses said he was unfit when God called him as leader of the Israelites. (Exodus 4:1ff) Jeremiah claimed he was too young when God called him to be a prophet. (Jeremiah 1:6) Jonah headed off in the opposite direction when God gave him a mission in Nineveh. (Jonah 1:3ff) As so many biblical people had done before her, Mary demonstrates that God does not call self-effacing doormats into His service. He summons real people with real questions, objections, doubts and fears. It was only human for Mary to have them, as it is only human that we have them, too.

Our text shows Mary joining another tradition as well, a long line of women in the Bible — foremothers of our faith — who were chosen by God for special duties. Some, like Deborah or Jael, were judges or military leaders. But within this tradition is a smaller group of women whom God chose to bring special children into the world. They include Sarah, the aged wife of Abraham, who became the "Mother of Nations" by bearing Isaac, (Genesis 8:12) and Rachel, the mother of Joseph. (Genesis 30:22) We have already mentioned Elizabeth, mother of John the Baptist. And then there was Mary.

These women were chosen for motherhood, but they were more than mere vessels for delivering children. They became interpreters of God's will, reflecting on their own experience of pregnancy and motherhood to understand how God works in the world.

This is precisely what we see in our Old Testament lesson, where we meet a woman named Hannah, who lived a thousand years before Mary was born. Now, Hannah had been barren all her life, despite years of praying and pleading for a child. She daily felt the shame of her childlessness from other women in a culture where fertility was considered a sign of God's favor.

Finally, God gave a very special child to Hannah; his name was Samuel and he became the last of Israel's great judges. Of course, Hannah was ecstatic, and our text shows her expressing her joy in words of praise: "My heart exults in the Lord," she says, "my strength is exalted in my God."

Then she goes on to interpret what her own particular story reveals about the purposes of God. The pregnancy of a forlorn, barren woman like her is a sign, she declares, that "The bows of the mighty are broken, [and] the feeble gird on strength." God "raises up the poor from the dust; He lifts the needy from the ash heap." This is God's way in the world, Hannah is saying, and the fact that God would favor with a child a downtrodden woman like her is living proof of it.

A thousand years later, Mary echoed Hannah's words as she interpreted her own situation in light of the methods, the mind and the will of God. By favoring a poor, obscure girl like her, Mary says, God has "scattered the proud in the imagination of their hearts." By passing over other women who possessed more wealth, prestige or comfort and choosing Mary instead, God has "brought down the mighty from their thrones and lifted up the lowly." By placing Himself among the poor and homeless, God has "filled the hungry with good things and sent the rich empty away."

Here is Mary — thoughtful, serene, obedient Mary — giving us the good news of Christ's birth in all its radical fullness! Here is Mary making sense of why God chose her among all women and explaining to the rest of us that when God's will is enacted in the world, He radically inverts our worldly values. When God's will is enacted in the world, the last become first and the first become last; the dishonored are exalted and the honored are humbled.

As we live by the ways of the world, honoring the rich and fawning over the famous, God comes to Bethlehem to honor the poor and bless the obscure. As we honor those with power and might, God comes to a stable to honor the powerless and the meek of the earth. As we honor all that is flashy and spectacular, God shows that His way is as humble as a manger and simple as a solitary star.

Did not the ancient prophet say, "For My thoughts are not your thoughts, neither are your ways My ways, says the Lord." (Isaiah 55:8) This is also the message of Mary's Magnificat, arising from her own reflection on her womanly experience as well as her knowledge of Old Testament scripture.

Mary was a woman of noble virtues, such as courage, obedience and humility. She had a mind of her own and even had her doubts, but she was willing to endure any hardship to do God's will. She stands in a long tradition of biblical women who interpreted God's ways to the world. Yet we can say all of this about Mary and still not reveal what is most important about her. What matters most about Mary is that she was a regular, ordinary person.

She declares as much in our text. "God has looked with favor upon the lowliness of His servant," she says. She is a simple peasant girl, engaged to a carpenter and living in a dusty little village in a dusty little nation. She never calls herself anything unique or special, never claims to be more educated, refined or worthy in any way than anyone else. In fact, Mary realizes that the glory which has come to her is all God's doing: "The Mighty One has done great things for me," she confesses. She will be blessed among women for all eternity because she was an ordinary, unspectacular girl who said "yes" to a spectacular calling from God.

There is an important spiritual lesson to be learned here, which is that God doesn't need people who are unusually strong or bright or well-to-do to be His servants. God doesn't need people who are exceptionally well-educated or skilled to do

His will — ordinary folks will do just fine. In fact, if you think about it for a moment, ordinary people are all God has to work with, so there is no reason for any of us to say no to His summons to service!

Like Mary and countless other servants before her and since, we think of all the reasons God can't be calling us to ministry in His name. We aren't good or deserving enough. We aren't faithful or religious enough. We don't have this, that or the other thing which would commend us to God or qualify us for His service.

The problem with this is that we assume too much of ourselves and too little of God when we think in those terms. We assume that God's work is always so monumental and earthshaking that we need special gifts or talents to be useful to Him, when the truth is that God doesn't need any of that from us! God doesn't need the strength of our flesh but the willingness of our spirit. God is so great and His power so glorious that all He needs is for average, everyday people like you and me to submit our wills to His.

Mary's soul magnified the Lord as she received God's Son and brought Him into the world, and she is venerated by Christians around the world because of it. In some branches of the church, it is even said that Mary, like Jesus Himself, was born sinlessly and ascended bodily up to heaven after she died.

All of that is well and good, and historically, those branches of the Christian church have had certain theological reasons for revering Mary in this way. I am not here to condemn any of that.

But perhaps we do Mary and ourselves a spiritual disservice if we put her on too high a pedestal, if we endow her with such superior qualities as to place her beyond the reach of our human nature. Mary is blessed among women today not because she was unusually able or radically different from anyone else, but because she was a simple, ordinary girl who allowed God's glory to shine through her. If she were any different — if she were somehow superhuman in some special sense — we would not have to challenge ourselves to be as faithful and obedient as she was. No, Mary was a simple, ordinary person in God's sight just as we are, which makes her life all the more inspiring and her story all the more compelling to Christians today. Amen.

## Pastoral Prayer

**God of wonder and God of light, we continue to stand in awe at the way You brought Your Son into the world, and we thank You for the ordinary people who helped You do it. In particular, we thank You for the service of Mary, whose courage, faith and thoughtful serenity continue to appeal to us today. We ask that the example she set inspire our own virtues, helping us to rise above the world's worship of self to follow Mary's higher path of humility, obedience and self-giving service.**

**Most of all, dear God, we ask that You put within our hearts a clear understanding of the service You desire from each one of us. While we are aware of our weaknesses, do not let that awareness excuse us from allowing Your divine strength to work through us. Make us more eager to say yes to Your will, that like Mary, we may gladly bear the cost of Your service until our souls are magnifying our Lord with power, purpose and praise forever. We ask this all in Jesus' name. Amen.**

# Tell God When
# You Are Happy

**Luke 1:39-56**
**"And Mary said, 'My soul magnifies the Lord, and
my spirit rejoices in God my Savior.' "**

**(vv. 46-47)**

Have you had any complaints lately at home, any situations in which you told your parents you didn't like something? Have you had to do something or eat something you didn't like lately? *(Let them answer.)*

That's right, you let your parents know what you thought of the creamed asparagus they made you eat, or how your bedtime is unfair because your friend down the street gets to stay up later. You may have mentioned once or twice (perhaps in a rather loud and insistent voice) that you didn't think you were dirty enough to take a bath. If you have brothers and sisters, I am sure you complained when your sister got three pieces of bacon and you only got two, or when your older brother got a new bike and you got the one he used to have.

Now let me ask you: have you ever told your parents when you are happy about something? Did you tell them you liked the dinner they cooked, or you appreciated the way they took time off from work to see your school play? When you have a wonderful day at school, or when everything just seems to be going right for you, do you come home and tell your parents all about it?

I'll bet you are much quicker to tell your parents when you are unhappy than when you are happy. For example, when you are playing with your friends, you don't come running to your parents just to tell them what a great time you are having. But if your friend knocks you down, or if you get into an argument about the rules of the game, you come running and screaming to your parents in a minute, right! Most people are like that — bad news is louder than good news.

The point is, we are the same way with God. We talk to God when we have problems, or when we are worried about something, or when we want something we do not have, and that is all well and good. It's perfectly all right to share our burdens with God and pray to Him when all is not well. But don't you think God also wants to hear from us when we are happy, too? Don't you think we can also talk to God when we are joyful and generally pleased with our lives?

That's what Mary did at the beginning of the Christmas story. When Mary learned that she was to give birth to Jesus, she was very happy. In fact, she was overjoyed, and the very first thing she did was tell God how she felt. She said, "My soul magnifies the Lord, and my spirit rejoices in God my Savior." ("My soul declares how great God is, and my spirit rejoices in God my Savior.") Just as parents love to hear from their children when they are glad, I am sure that Mary's prayer of joy pleased God as well.

Long after Christmas is over and the presents are all unwrapped, there will be other things to make you glad in the year ahead. So remember Mary and take her example to heart. Don't just tell God when you are sad or upset about something; tell God when you are happy as well. Amen.

# Merry
# Kurtzman

Once upon a time, in a land far, far away, there was a wee, small country the rest of the world had never heard of called Cornucopia. It was a beautiful little country with sparkling cities and quaint rural towns, lush, rolling hills and rich farmland fed by streams of the cleanest water you ever saw. It was a prosperous country as well, where even the poorest of Cornucopians felt blessed with "the good life" and considered themselves better off than most other people in the world.

People sometimes wondered how an idyllic little country like this could remain largely unnoticed by the rest of the world, but it really isn't so mysterious! You see, no one from Cornucopia ever wanted to leave, and the few visitors who did come quickly decided that they wanted to stay. In this way, Cornucopia went on quietly about its business year after year, generation after generation, with minimal interference from the rest of the human race.

One day, two visitors came to Cornucopia, wearing backpacks and hiking right down the main street of the capital city. Of course, the Cornucopians recognized right away that they were strangers and greeted them warmly. "Merry Kurtzman!" they said as they passed by on the street. "Merry Kurtzman!" the children shouted as they raced along the sidewalk, and when the visitors entered a hotel to get a room, even the clerk at the desk greeted them with a cheery, "Merry Kurtzman! How may I help you?"

"Tell us what this 'Merry Kurtzman' means," the visitors asked. "Why, everyone knows about Kurtzman Day!" the clerk replied in astonishment. Looking at the visitors' blank faces, the hotel clerk shrugged her shoulders. "Well, you'll soon find out," she remarked with a smile. "You're really quite lucky, you know. You have come to Cornucopia just in time for the biggest holiday of the year! Only one more day until Kurtzman!" she said as she left the front desk and went back into her office.

After checking into their room, the visitors went strolling through the capital city. Every window had a Kurtzman candle in it, along with elaborately decorated pictures of a rather jolly looking man whom the visitors presumed to be Mr. Kurtzman himself. Some of the stores and businesses had gone to great expense, arranging thousands of brightly colored lights in fabulous holiday displays. "Whoever this Kurtzman guy is," one of the visitors said to the other, "he sure is important to the merchants."

As the two visitors continued their walk through the capital city, they saw that it wasn't just the merchants, but everyone in Cornucopia who got into the Kurtzman spirit. School lessons were stopped so the children could gather in the auditorium and put on Kurtzman plays for audiences of delighted parents. Radio stations played Kurtzman music, friends threw Kurtzman parties and drug stores were filled with Kurtzman cards of every description.

Even the churches were filled to capacity during the Kurtzman season. In fact, right in the center of the city was the largest church in Cornucopia — a huge, sprawling edifice called "The First Church of Kurtzman." It was an imposing structure of steel and glass with a huge wooden "K" on the roof which pointed upward to the heavens. Hordes of people were gathering up their money and streaming into this church, so the two visitors followed, curious to learn about this man named Kurtzman who inspired such devotion.

As they got their first look inside, their eyes opened wide with wonder. There before them was an enormous sanctuary with bright lights and shimmering chandeliers. The room was so large that benches were placed throughout the open space to allow tired people a place to sit. Surrounding the sanctuary on every side were rows of smaller stores and boutiques as far as the eye could see, each one glittering with merchandise and filled with people.

Soothing music was wafting through the church, but no one seemed to pay attention to it. In fact, the whole church was filled with frantic activity as people rushed in every direction, jostling and elbowing each other aside, trying to be the first to reach the strategically placed check-out altars. Some put real money on the counter and others used little pieces of plastic, but everyone was in a hurry to make their offering to this man named Kurtzman.

Having seen how the entire country was in an uproar over Kurtzman Day, the two visitors decided they had to find out more about it. That night, they approached the hotel clerk and inquired where they might meet the esteemed Mr. Kurtzman. "Regis Kurtzman?" the clerk exclaimed with a laugh. "Why, you can't meet him now; he lived 2,000 years ago. But we believe he is still here as an inspiration for everyone who has the Kurtzman spirit."

"Then, who was he," the visitors asked, "and what is this so-called Kurtzman spirit all about?" "Well, Regis Kurtzman was only the greatest man who ever lived," the clerk sniffed, "and today we worship him like a king. I'm amazed you haven't heard about him!"

"Regis Kurtzman," she began, "was born on the 25th of December a long, long time ago in a rustic little inn. Mind you, he wasn't born in a big, fancy five-star hotel downtown, but in a small one-star placed called The Manger Inn on the outskirts of town. His mother's name was Sherry and his father's name was Rudolph."

"Little Regis was born very poor, but when he grew up he founded a toy company which became the biggest in the world. He had stores in every town and sold every toy under the sun. Every child in the world wanted to join his Kurtzman Kids Clubs, and they knew all the Kurtzman commercials by heart."

59

"But being a successful businessman wasn't enough for Regis Kurtzman, and one day he decided to do something which would make everyone in the whole world happy. He decided that every year on his birthday — December 25th — he would dress up in a bright red suit and deliver Kurtzman toys to children through the world. All year long, children would make out their Kurtzman lists and tell him what they wanted, and if they had been good, he would give it to them. It was a wonderful idea; that's why you saw so many people in the church-malls today," the clerk continued. "They were all buying gifts in order to get into the Kurtzman spirit."

"But no one looks very happy during the Kurtzman season," the two visitors said. "We watched them in that huge church downtown, and everyone looked so harried and tired! They were climbing all over each other at the check-out altars, acting like they just had too many things to do. In fact, we remarked to each other that you Cornucopians don't seem to celebrate Kurtzman Day so much as try to survive it. Even the children seem anxious about Kurtzman Day, wondering if they will get what they want."

"Well, you do have a point there," the hotel clerk replied. "The Kurtzman season does seem to get more exhausting and more expensive all the time. We know it will be like this each year, but what can we do? After all, the Good Book says this is what we must do on December 25th to honor the birth of Regis Kurtzman."

"You have a book that tells all about Mr. Kurtzman?" the visitors asked. "Why yes, it's our sacred scripture," the clerk replied. "It's been quite a while since I've looked at it myself, but I'll see if I can find it for you."

Almost an hour later, the clerk returned with a large, heavy leather-bound book. "Here it is," she said as she blew the dust off the cover and handed it to her inquisitive visitors. They opened to the title page and almost dropped the book in surprise. "Why, this is the Holy Bible!" they exclaimed, and as they thumbed through the pages, they discovered it was the same Bible they knew. "You think this book is about Regis Kurtzman?" they asked. "When was the last time you read it?"

"Like I said, it's been a while," the clerk replied without embarrassment. "In fact, no one in Cornucopia actually reads this book any more — we all know the story by heart, and we've handed it down by word of mouth from generation to generation."

Suddenly the two visitors understood what had happened. "Have you ever played a game," they asked the clerk, "where one person tells a secret to another person, and that person tells the next person, and by the time it reaches the last one in line, the secret has been changed completely?"

"Well, that's what you people in Cornucopia have done. As you passed on the story down through the years, the pronunciation of the words slowly changed, then the story itself gradually changed, and no one realized it because no one went back to the source and read the book. Now the story is so distorted that you don't have a clue what this holiday season is really about!"

"It's not Kurtzman Day you should celebrate, it's *Christmas* Day and the name isn't Regis Kurtzman but Jesus Christ. Furthermore, Jesus wasn't born in a one-star place called the Manger Inn; He was born *under* a shining star *in* a manger because *there was no room for Him* at the inn. And His parents weren't Sherry and Rudolph; His mother was Mary and his father's name was Joseph."

"Most importantly, Jesus Christ doesn't flit around door to door giving presents to children who are good; that's not what the Christmas spirit is really about! The true Christmas spirit is a feeling of joy and gratitude that Jesus Christ was born to bring us love and peace and forgiveness of sins, to show us how to live in God's ways in service to one another, to show us how to live for God and the things that really matter in life."

"Haven't you wondered why your Kurtzman season is so exhausting and joyless for so many people? It's because you have allowed material gifts which delight only for a moment to become the entire reason for the season. You need to learn about spiritual gifts which come from above, because once you possess those gifts, your joy will be complete and will never leave you.''

The hotel clerk asked the visitors to stop for a moment, while she gathered more people to listen to them. Then the two visitors began to tell the people of Cornucopia the story of Jesus Christ: how He was promised by prophets of old, how He was born, the way He lived, the things He taught, the sacrifice He made upon the cross and how He was raised again. The people were spellbound, realizing that this was a far richer, more meaningful story than the one they had been telling all these years. They all went looking for their Holy Bibles in order to learn more.

A few days later, the people of Cornucopia had a meeting. They decided they would keep the Kurtzman holiday, since the children loved it so and it mattered so much to the Cornucopian economy. But they promised never again to let the materialism of Kurtzman Day become more important than the spiritual meaning of Christmas Day. They promised they would never again stray so far from scripture as to forget the story of their salvation. They would learn this new and deeper joy which does not end when the presents are opened, but lasts instead throughout the year. That is just what they did, and that is how it literally became true that the people of Cornucopia lived happily ever after. Amen.

### Pastoral Prayer

**O Good and Faithful God, who has led us here on this most wondrous night of the year, we thank You for all that makes this season so special. We thank You for the expectant eyes of little children who eagerly anticipate the coming dawn. We thank You for the warmth of family and friends who gather to share their love at this time of year. We give You**

thanks for the spirit which is in this church tonight, reflected in faces which shine by flickering candlelight and hearts which sing for joy at the coming of our Lord.

O God of love and justice, we pray that the light which shines in Your church tonight will illuminate the world as well. Let the Light of our Lord brighten every lonely heart and quicken every troubled spirit. We ask most fervently that the Light of Your divine love dispel the dark clouds of war and injustice which shadow so much of this planet, that the day soon may come when all the earth is basking in the bright sunshine of equity and peace. Most of all, dear God, we ask that You be present with those who are poor and homeless on this Christmas Eve, for tonight as in that Bethlehem stable so long ago, it is among the least of these, Your children, that Christ our Savior is born. Amen.

# Is There Life After Christmas?

**Isaiah 12:1-6; Luke 2:21-35**
**"This child is destined ... to be a sign that is op-**
**posed, so that the inner thoughts of many will be**
**revealed."**                                    **(Luke 2:34b)**

During his tenure as head football coach at the University of Arkansas, Lou Holtz once had his team play a bowl game on Christmas Day. When a reporter asked him how he felt about playing football on this day, rather than being at home with his family, Coach Holtz was honest and to the point. "Frankly, I'd rather be doing this," he said. "Once you've been to church, had dinner and opened the gifts, Christmas is the most boring day of the year."

Is there life after Christmas or is Lou Holtz right? Is there anything to do, anything to look forward to once the big day has come and gone, or is the aftermath of Christmas merely, as Lou Holtz might say, the most "boring" time of the year?

It is not uncommon to feel a certain let down after Christmas — we even do it in the church. After all, what is the slowest, lowest, most anticlimactic Sunday of the year? Or, to put the matter on a more practical level we can understand: on which Sunday can you come to church five minutes late and not have to worry about finding a parking space? If it isn't the Sunday after Easter, it is surely the Sunday after Christmas!

Traditionally on this day, worship attendance plummets, and the energy level we had during Advent seems to dissipate

64

as well. It's as if we collectively use this time to rest, catch our breath and say, "Whew! Christmas is over — thank God that is done with! Now we have nothing to worry about until Easter."

Parents of newborn babies know otherwise. When the child is safely delivered, the mother relaxes in exhausted happiness and the father beams with pride and joy, but the respite after the birth only lasts a moment. Now that the baby is here, she needs food and warm clothing. She needs love expressed in a close embrace, and soon she will need her diapers changed for the first of many times. Lest we forget, newborn babies quickly remind us with their numerous needs that our lives as parents have only begun.

Fortunately, we have this morning's text from Luke to give us the same lesson with respect to our lives as Christians. We may wonder if there is life (or life in the church) after Christmas, but our text shows us that for Joseph and Mary, life did go on.

Besides their familiar parental duties, Mary and Joseph also attend to their religious duties in the days following Christmas. They had Jesus circumcised eight days after his birth, as the law commanded. (Genesis 17:10-12) Again according to law, Mary underwent a rite of purification, (Leviticus 12:2f) since mothers were considered ritually unclean after the birth of a child.

Then, at the proper time, Joseph and Mary presented Jesus at the temple in Jerusalem, where He was dedicated to God in accordance with scripture. (Exodus 13:1-2) They also offered their temple sacrifice of "two turtledoves or two pigeons," which the law allowed as a substitution when parents were too poor to afford a sacrificial lamb. (Leviticus 12:8) Four times in this short text, Luke says that Joseph and Mary performed their religious duties as Jewish law required in the aftermath of Jesus' birth.

As it does for us today, life went on after Christmas for Joseph and Mary, including worship and the practice of their faith. They did this all the time and not just on the one or

65

two most holy days of the year. They (and we) are to be commended for that.

But even as Joseph and Mary are fulfilling the law at the temple, they meet an old man named Simeon, who speaks from the Holy Spirit in words which comfort and disturb, revealing that the spiritual significance of this child's life will go far beyond the observance of religious rituals. Simeon promises that this newborn baby, who looks so helpless and unassuming right now, will someday grow up to be a unique Man with a singular destiny for all people.

"This child is destined for the falling and rising of many in Israel," Simeon says, foreshadowing the controversies which would follow Jesus throughout His ministry. Many will fall and rise in the new covenant which Jesus will establish in His body and blood.

By the Word of this child, those who are proud and convinced of their worthiness in God's sight shall fall, while those who are poor in spirit and who know their need for God's mercy shall rise and receive the kingdom of heaven. (cf. Matthew 5:3ff)

Because of this child and all He means, those who are happy and who seem to have things going their way in the world shall fall, while those who mourn shall rise and be comforted.

Those who are privileged and arrogant in power, who swagger through society, scattering lesser mortals before them and making self-serving rules for others to live by shall fall, while those who are meek shall rise and inherit the earth.

Those who are complacent about all that is wrong in the world, who tolerate injustice and unrighteousness in the name of immutable "laws" of human nature shall fall, while those who hunger and thirst for what is right shall rise and be filled.

Those who commit the obscenity of war, who use instruments of destruction against their neighbors shall fall, while those who are peacemakers shall rise and be called the children of God.

Those who bask in the glory and honor of popular acclaim, who lead respectable lives in conformity to the canons of culture shall fall, while those who are rejected and persecuted for righteousness' sake shall rise and enter the kingdom of heaven.

This child shall grow "from his roots" with "the Spirit of the Lord upon Him," and with all His "counsel and might," He will not judge as the world judges, by what the eye sees and the ear hears. He will not judge the worthiness or usefulness of others by their wealth, their power or their standing in public opinion polls. He will not judge as priest or profiteer or politician are apt to judge, but "with righteousness He shall judge the poor, and decide with equity for the meek of the earth." He will judge by God's standards — not the world's standards — and therefore, many who expect to rise shall fall, and many who expect to fall shall rise.

All of this, says Simeon, shall make this child "a sign that will be opposed." Imagine that: God's Son, born in a humble manger, will become so threatening as to be opposed in the world by the cruelest of means! Even today, as we remember the beauty of Bethlehem, we forget that the path of Jesus' life leads to Calvary!

"He was in the world ... yet the world knew Him not. He came to what was His own, and His own people received Him not." (John 1:10-11) He was rejected then, and we who are His own people reject Him even now, as we restrict His claim upon our lives, as we keep our faith within manageable and reasonable limits, as we remain beholden to the world, using almost all of our time, our talents and especially our money for ourselves and not for Him.

Today, we look at newborn babies and wonder what the future holds for them, but Simeon knew as he looked at Christ; that's why Simeon spoke of "a sign to be opposed" and "the falling and rising of many." This child, who is God's "light" and "glory," shall nonetheless be "despised and rejected ... a man of sorrows." (Isaiah 53:3) It will not be an easy life, for Jesus or His mother. "A sword will pierce your own soul too," Simeon says quietly to Mary.

In the final analysis, declares Simeon, this child will become a Man who causes "the inner thoughts of many to be revealed." He will become a dividing line — a divining line — by which lives are tested and hearts are measured. By His life, death and resurrection, Jesus will present to each of us the only essential choice we must make in life: will we go against the grain of worldly convention to follow our Lord, or will we stay on the safe side of conformity? We reveal the thoughts of our hearts when we come down on one side or the other of that line. (Matthew 25:31ff)

Whether we perceive it, we reveal our inner thoughts all the time, by every action we take or fail to take. When we stop to help a stranded motorist — or drive by and ignore his need — we reveal ourselves in ways more profound than we realize. When we speak callously of the poor or stand up to defend the poor even when it is unfashionable to do so, we reveal ourselves again, along with our values and the inner thoughts of our hearts.

It is even more true with Jesus. We can only choose to live for or against Him — there is no middle way. We can only choose to be His disciple or His detractor, and if we choose the former, we choose a set of principles and a way of life which Simeon knows are bitterly opposed by the world. There is no mystery to that, nor is it a mystery to God or anyone else which choice we make. Our values, our priorities and our lifestyles all reveal to God and the world the content of our hearts and the character of our souls.

What will we try to do with our lives, and who or what will we try to serve? How often we end up like a character named Mathilde in Guy de Maupassant's story, *The Necklace* — the story of a woman who was married to an ordinary citizen but who wanted more than anything to hobnob with French high society.

One day, her husband received an invitation to a high society ball. Excited to finally realize her dream, Mathilde borrowed a friend's expensive necklace to wear for the occasion.

The beautiful necklace drew admiring comments from many of the guests at the ball, but as luck would have it, Mathilde lost the necklace before the night was over. Panic-stricken, she and her husband borrowed 36,000 francs, bought an exact duplicate of the necklace and returned it to her friend without telling her what happened.

For 10 painful years, the couple slaved away in toil and hardship. They sold their house, dismissed their servants and worked two jobs in order to repay their enormous debt.

When they finally did pay off the debt, Mathilde told her friend about the replacement necklace and how they had suffered the last 10 years. That is when the friend told her that the necklace Mathilde had borrowed that night was itself an imitation, made only of paste. It was barely worth 500 francs, not the 36,000 they had slaved so long to repay.

Of course, there is a part of Mathilde in all of us. We spend years slaving away for things which are only made of paste, while failing to see the "pearls of great value" (Matthew 13:46) which are staring us in the face — pearls of faith, hope and love, forgiveness, joy and peace, Christ's salvation and eternal life.

Simeon comes along to remind us that there is, indeed, life after Christmas. The baby Jesus does grow up. He does fulfill His destiny for the falling and rising of many. He does become a sign which is opposed on earth while pointing to glory in heaven.

Now that He is born, Jesus reduces all of our choices in life to one — to live with Him or without Him. To live as Christians "in an alien land," (Psalm 137:4) or to live as people who are "conformed to this world." (Romans 12:2) On this Sunday after Christmas and the final Sunday of the year, it is a good time to think about this choice, to reflect on what it says about the rest of our outward lives, and what it reveals about the innermost thoughts of our hearts as well. Amen.

## Pastoral Prayer

Most Pure and Righteous God, whose Son is born in our midst, not to end the story of our salvation but to begin it, we ask that You help us find our way during these days and weeks after Christmas. Do not let us linger too long in Bethlehem, with its holy mystery and humble majesty, but as with Mary and Joseph so long ago, remind us that life goes on and send us on our way. Do not let us linger too long over a newborn Jesus, but lead us forward to face the Man this baby will become. Help us to measure our lives by His, and give us the courage to choose His way of life for our own. Let our choice for Him reveal thoughts in our hearts which are pleasing to You, that each of us alone and all of us together may be Your people, witnesses to Your love and recipients of Your grace. In Jesus' name. Amen.

# What Are You Looking Forward To?

**Luke 2:21-35**
**"Now there was a man in Jerusalem whose name was Simeon; this man was righteous and devout, looking forward to the consolation of Israel, and the Holy Spirit rested on Him."** (v. 25)

Now that Christmas is over, do you have anything to look forward to? Is there anything coming up that will make you happy and excited, or do you think that's all over with now that Christmas has come and gone?

Vacation will be over and school will be starting again in a week or so. Are you looking forward to going back to school? *(Let them answer.)* Pretty soon, you will be reading stories and doing math and taking tests again. Does that make you excited? But before you do that, you'll have to take all the Christmas clothes you got that don't fit or don't match and spend five hours with your mother in the clothing store trying on different sizes and colors. Are you looking forward to that? Now that Christmas is over, what are you looking forward to?

Of course, there are some good things to look forward to as you think a little further ahead. In just half a year, summer vacation will be here, and you will have lots of time to play. And sometime between now and next Christmas, you'll have a birthday party — those are two good things to look forward to, right?

Think a little further ahead. In just a few years, you will be old enough to get a driver's license. Won't that be nice?

Further down the road, you can look forward to finishing school, finding some work that you like, perhaps getting married and having children. There's a lot to look forward to in life, isn't there?

The Bible tells us that a week after Jesus was born, His mother and father took Him to Jerusalem, where they met a man named Simeon, who talked with them and gave them a blessing. Now Simeon was very old, so he may have felt he didn't have a lot left to look forward to in life. Or he may have been content to look forward to his retirement, to taking it easy, visiting with his grandchildren and enjoying his memories. But the Bible says that Simeon was actually looking forward "to the consolation of Israel," which means he was looking forward to the coming of Jesus Christ. He wanted to see Jesus face to face, to know the Son of God in the flesh and draw near to Him. When he did this, Simeon felt his life was complete.

What are you looking forward to? You can look forward to school and growing up, and as you get older, you can look forward to grandchildren, retirement or many other good things. But Simeon reminds us that there is much more to seek in life, and we ought not set our sights too low. We can look forward to knowing God more and more as we grow older, to growing closer to God in every way we can. We can look forward to knowing Jesus, and to living with Him more closely as the years go by. Like Simeon, we can grow in spirit and wisdom because we are looking forward to something much larger than ourselves. So, if ever you should be asked what you are looking forward to, tell them you are looking forward to knowing your God, to living more closely with your God, and to drawing so near to Him as to see Him face to face. Amen.

# The Flight
# From Light

**Isaiah 60:1-5; Matthew 2:1-12**
**"And being warned in a dream not to return to Herod, they departed to their own country by another way."** **(Matthew 2:12)**

The other day I called someone to compliment her on a job she had done exceedingly well. We had worked on a project together which became a great success, in no small part because of the leadership she provided. As I spoke with her, I went on and on about how much her work had been appreciated. "Everyone who was there really loved you," I told her; "in fact, they're raving about you!" Then I added, "Of course, I don't know what they see in you myself, but they all seemed to be impressed anyway."

It was a joke, and she took it as a joke. "That's right," she laughed, "don't let me get a swelled head about this!" A few minutes later, the conversation was over.

After I hung up the phone, I started thinking: when we experience a high moment like this, a moment of real success and appreciation, why do we feel we have to poke fun at it or cut it off? When we feel like bursting with happiness and enthsuiasm about something that has gone well, when we find ourselves on one of life's rare mountaintops of joy and grace, why do we feel a need to puncture the mood and rush back down into the valley again, as if we are afraid the good feeling might last too long?

Our texts show something like this happening after the birth of Jesus. "Arise, shine; for your light has come," cries Isaiah. After suffering for all of human history in a thick, oppressive darkness which has covered the earth and all its people, God's light has finally come! More than that, it has come for everyone and not just a chosen few. With Epiphany, the light which came to a little town called Bethlehem is now being given to all the world.

You would think the world would rejoice. But in Matthew, we see that rather than welcoming this light and flocking to it, the world is fleeing from it. In fact, Herod is trying to destroy it.

It is the light of justice and compassion, a light which dispels the darkness of indifferent greed and responds with love to human need, a light which "judges the poor with righteousness and decides with equity for the meek of the earth." (Isaiah 11:4)

It is also the light of peace. It is a light which disperses the dense darkness of violence and aggression which have bedeviled us for so long and empties out once and for all the boiling caldrons of war. Since the dawn of time, what has humanity yearned for more feverently than peace? What has humanity been more tragically confused about than the methods and means of achieving peace? Now, at long last, a light has come into the world to end our confusion, to be our peace (Ephesians 2:14) and to show us in the flesh "the things that make for peace." (Luke 19:42)

Here is a light which can answer the deepest longings of the human heart, and Herod is alarmed. Here is a light of new hope in a world whose long, dark history has been written in blood, and Herod is terrified. In fact, he is so unnerved at the prospect of a different kind of ruler and a new kingdom of justice and peace that he orders a terrible massacre in Bethlehem. The violence always falls indiscriminately on the innocent as the thick darkness descends, and a perennial "voice is heard in Ramah," the sound of Rachel weeping for her children "because they are no more." (Matthew 2:18)

Of course, we aren't talking about just one brutal, first-century dictator here; there are Herods in every era and nation who fear and despise the light. In every age, we think we want a world of justice and peace, but when we are confronted with the possibility of actually approaching it, and when we are shown how to create the conditions which nurture it, we turn away from that light and settle back into the familiar darkness. Believe in this new king, O Herods of the earth! Live in His way, love with His love, rule in His light and you will see peace in your time! The prospect frightens Herods everywhere. Why do you think that is?

Actually, a closer reading of our text tells all of us to answer that question, because it isn't just the Herods in positions of power who fear that this light might end the darkness — our text says that "all of Jerusalem" was frightened as well. Every citizen, great and small! Each one of us today! In one way or another, we all turn and flee from the light of the very things we think we want the most.

What do we want the most, you and I? What do we most desire, not in the sense of a thing to be bought but a quality which would make us whole? Think about what you really want, and then think about what you do when faced with the prospect of actually getting it.

One thing we want is companionship, an end to our loneliness. In some ways, we have it with friends and loved ones, but in other ways we are all too aware of our solitude. We come into this world alone and leave it alone, and in between those two events we are searching for connection.

To whom can we really talk, and who is there to really listen? Who can hear our deepest secrets and not think badly of us for telling them? Who is there to know us through and through — all that is good, bad and ugly about us — and love us just the same?

We want to be cared for, listened to, understood and appreciated. We are searching for the intimacy of understanding, body to body and soul to soul, but when we come to the brink of real sharing and genuine communion, we back away.

75

When we come to the brink of one searching person deeply touching another searching person with honest love and fearless truth, we retreat and raise our guard. We practice the art of remaining strangers. In ways we may or may not recognize, we are continually fleeing from the light of caring and sharing into the lonely darkness again, desperately wanting communion with others but afraid to open our hearts and be vulnerable, afraid to expose ourselves or admit our need.

We also want our wounds to be healed, an end to our pain. Sometimes our pain is physical, ranging in severity from the distracting to the debilitating, and we wish we were free of it. More often, our pain is emotional, psychological and spiritual. Each of us is wounded in more ways than we can count or understand.

We are wounded by dramatic, specific events in our lives which leave lasting scars: a shattering loss here, a twist of fate there. We are also wounded in more elusive ways by the ebb and flow of life itself. As children, we are wounded by the families which raised us; no matter how much our parents may have loved or cared for us, they were coping with wounds they had received as children, so the pain is handed down, often unintentionally, like unwanted inheritances from generation to generation.

As adults, we are wounded by the families we ourselves raise, wounded by spouses and children even in the most loving of homes, We are wounded at work and in the world by faceless alienation, wounded almost daily by betrayals large and small. We are wounded as dreams die and cherished life goals are adjusted to fit reality.

We want our wounds healed, but when we come face to face with the cause of our pain, we avert our eyes and deny what we see. When the prescription for ending our soul's distress is placed in our hands, we dare not take it to our lips. To be sure, we do not like the darkness which holds our hurts and pains, but we are afraid to let it go, so we go on living with our brokenness, yearning to be whole.

Finally, we want communion with God. The answer to our loneliness and pain is communion with God, and we yearn for it with all our might. But when the moment comes and God is ready to fill us, we shut Him out. When God confronts us with the possibility of giving up whatever it is that is keeping us in darkness, we cling all the more fiercely to it and run fearfully from the light.

When I send my young children to the basement to get something for me, they say they cannot go because they are afraid of the dark. They beg me to leave a light on when they go to sleep. In our corporal lives, we fear darkness and crave light. But in our spiritual lives — in those intensely personal dramas which are played out in the privacy of our hearts and the sanctuary of our souls — our attitudes toward darkness and light are frequently reversed. Our spiritual lives often amount to a reluctant embrace of darkness and a headlong flight from light.

The ancient Greek writer, Euripides, understood this human tragedy when he wrote, "People somehow fend off righteousness." *(Hippolytus 93)* What a phrase that is! Righteousness seeks us out and we actually fend it off! The apostle Paul knew this well: "I do not understand my own actions. For I do not do what I want, but I do the very thing I hate." (Romans 7:15) Who among us would deny that Paul is speaking for all of us and not just for himself?

Besides telling us that people flee the light which Christ brings into the world, our text also gives a hint as to why this is so. Notice that after they came and saw the infant Jesus, the wise men returned home to their own country "by another way." They had to make a change and take a route which was less familiar.

Is it really the darkness we love, or is it that we love what is familiar? When the Israelites were in the wilderness after escaping from Egypt, they rebelled against Moses and wanted to return to slavery. (Exodus 16) It wasn't that they loved slavery, for well they remembered how harsh their lives had been in Egypt. But slavery was familiar to them; at least they knew what their life would be like and what would happen day to day. Now that they were out in the wilderness, they had to trust in God for their sustenance, and their future was completely unknown. They wanted to escape from their freedom.

So it is with every torment, every addiction and dependency, every hurt and fear which enslaves our spirits today. How often do we cling to the things which keep us in darkness, thinking we are better off staying on the dead-end path we are accustomed to as opposed to trying a new and unfamiliar road? It takes courage to come home by a different route, and sometimes we prefer to stay with the sadness and darkness we know rather than leap sight unseen into the light of unfamiliar joy.

There once was an impoverished widow who had fallen badly behind on her bills. Her utilities had been cut off and the eviction notice had been received. She waited in fear for the inevitable.

One day, there was a knock on the door and the widow cowered in silence, keeping her doors locked and her curtains drawn. She trembled in terror as she heard the knock again, and then a third time. Finally, she allowed herself a silent sigh of relief as the knocking stopped and the sound of retreating footsteps grew dim.

She had assumed that the person knocking was the sheriff, coming to repossess her belongings and put her on the street. Had she found the courage to answer the door, she would have seen that her pastor was there, not the sheriff. Her pastor had come to tell her that he had raised enough money from her friends to catch up on her rent and pay off all her bills.

In some way, we are all like that frightened widow, cowering inside the dark houses of our private loneliness and pain, unaware that what we fear has actually come near to save us. King Herod's fierce political resistance to the light is merely a more graphic side of our own personal and spiritual resistance. The great irony of our religious life (if we are honest enough to admit it) is that even as we fear the darkness and praise the coming of God's light to the world, we spend much of our lives fleeing from the very light we think we are so fervently seeking.

At this very moment even as I speak, winds of pain are blowing through the world, and through our hearts as well. The pain within and the pain without are connected, as wind itself is indivisible. But listen! The One who is our light has come, and now He is knocking at our door. We think about fleeing deeper into the unrewarding comfort of familiar darkness, but He is knocking again. The time has come to arise and open the door, and let His light shine in. Amen.

### Pastoral Prayer

**Most Holy and Loving God, who saw the thick darkness under which Your children were languishing and did not abandon us there, we thank You for sending Your light in the form of this infant child named Jesus. We thank You that now we may live with supreme confidence and hope, certain beyond a doubt that a light will shine in our lives and in this troubled world which no amount of darkness can overcome. Teach us to seek Your light and not to flee it. Help us overcome our fear that Your light will change us and make us eager for that transformation. Loosen the grip which darkness has upon us, that our deepest yearnings may yet be realized as we walk in communion with our Lord in the light of His love. In Jesus' name, we pray. Amen.**

Children's Lesson For
Epiphany Sunday

# Your Light
# Has Come

**Isaiah 60;1-5**
**"Arise, shine; for your light has come, and the glory**
**of the Lord has risen upon you."** **(v. 1)**

How many of you are afraid of the dark? *(Let them answer.)* Are you afraid to sleep with the light off? Don't be embarrassed to admit it! It will be our little secret, just between you and me.

What is it that scares you about the dark? *(Let them answer.)* Maybe it's the way an ordinary thing in your room like a basketball hoop or a lamp or a large doll can look like a scary monster in the shadows of your vivid imaginations. Maybe it's the way you lie in the dark and think about something scary you saw on television or in a movie. Maybe it's the way your house or apartment is quiet when it is dark, which means that you can hear every little noise at night. Maybe you just don't feel safe because you can't see, and that is what makes the dark so scary.

Well, most people stop being afraid of the dark as they get older, but there is another kind of darkness which scares even grown-ups. I am talking about moral darkness, the darkness of wrong and evil. There is a lot of that darkness in the world, and it is scary because it keeps us from God. Young and old alike, we all must struggle to know and do what is right, to see and follow the light of good amid the darkness of what is bad.

Today we celebrate Epiphany and talk about how the light of God appeared in the world when Christ was born and made known to the world. The three wise men who visited the baby Jesus were among the first to see this light, but people had talked about it many centuries before. In fact, an ancient Hebrew prophet named Isaiah had written, "Arise, shine, for your light has come." Elsewhere, he had written, "The people who walked in darkness have seen a great light; those who lived in a land of deep darkness — on them light has shined." (9:2) For all people who were lost in darkness and couldn't find their way to God, Jesus has come to be their light and show us the way.

When you wake up from a bad dream in the middle of the night, think of how happy you are when your mother comes into your room and turns on the light. Then, after you have calmed down, she leaves the light on, and you aren't scared any more. That's sort of how we all feel now that Jesus is in the world. The light of goodness and salvation has been turned on in our souls, and we who were walking in darkness have seen the light. We aren't scared anymore.

Whenever you are tempted to do or say something you know is wrong, you are getting ready to enter this moral darkness I am talking about. It isn't a darkness you can see, like the night is dark; instead, it is a darkness inside which tries to take you away from God. But now we have Jesus Christ to be our light. Whenever we wonder what is the right or wrong thing to do, we have the example of Jesus to show us the right. Learn the stories of His life. Learn the stories He told and the lessons He taught; talk to your parents about Him. The thick darkness which has covered the peoples no longer is quite so thick or scary, because now that Jesus Christ is in the world, we see that our light has come. Amen.